D1506150

HOW DOES IT WORK?
TRAINS

by Nikole Brooks Bethea

Ideas for Parents and Teachers

Pogo Books let children practice reading informational text while introducing them to nonfiction features such as headings, labels, sidebars, maps, and diagrams, as well as a table of contents, glossary, and index.

Carefully leveled text with a strong photo match offers early fluent readers the support they need to succeed.

Before Reading

- "Walk" through the book and point out the various nonfiction features. Ask the student what purpose each feature serves.
- Look at the glossary together. Read and discuss the words.

Read the Book

- Have the child read the book independently.
- Invite him or her to list questions that arise from reading.

After Reading

- Discuss the child's questions. Talk about how he or she might find answers to those questions.
- Prompt the child to think more. Ask: What did you know about trains before you read this book? What more do you want to learn after reading it?

Pogo Books are published by Jump!
5357 Penn Avenue South
Minneapolis, MN 55419
www.jumplibrary.com

Library of Congress Cataloging-in-Publication Data

Names: Bethea, Nikole Brooks.
Title: Trains / by Nikole Brooks Bethea.
Description: Minneapolis, MN : Jump!, Inc., [2018]
Series: How does it work? | Audience: Ages 7-10.
Identifiers: LCCN 2017034524 (print)
LCCN 2017036509 (ebook)
ISBN 9781624967009 (ebook)
ISBN 9781620319123 (hardcover : alk. paper)
ISBN 9781620319130 (pbk.)
Subjects: LCSH: Railroad trains—Juvenile literature.
High speed trains—Juvenile literature.
Classification: LCC TF148 (ebook)
LCC TF148 .B4594 2018 (print) | DDC 625.2–dc23
LC record available at https://lccn.loc.gov/2017034524

Editor: Jenna Trnka
Book Designer: Leah Sanders
Photo Researcher: Leah Sanders

Photo Credits: victoriaKh/Shutterstock, cover; Ron Ellis/Shutterstock, 1; Scanrail1/Shutterstock, 3; Tim Boyle/Getty, 4; Leonid Andronov/Shutterstock, 5, 14-15; jgorzynik/Shutterstock, 6-7; Gudella/iStock, 8-9; John Kirk/iStock, 10; Albert Pego/Shutterstock, 11; Supannee_Hickman/Shutterstock, 12-13; OTHK/Getty, 16; joyfull/Shutterstock, 17; Christian Petersen-Clausen/Getty, 18-19; dpa picture alliance/Alamy, 20-21; A. and I. Kruk/Shutterstock, 23.

Printed in the United States of America at Corporate Graphics in North Mankato, Minnesota.

TABLE OF CONTENTS

CHAPTER 1

EARLY TRAINS

A loud horn blows in the distance. Crossing gates lower. A train roars by!

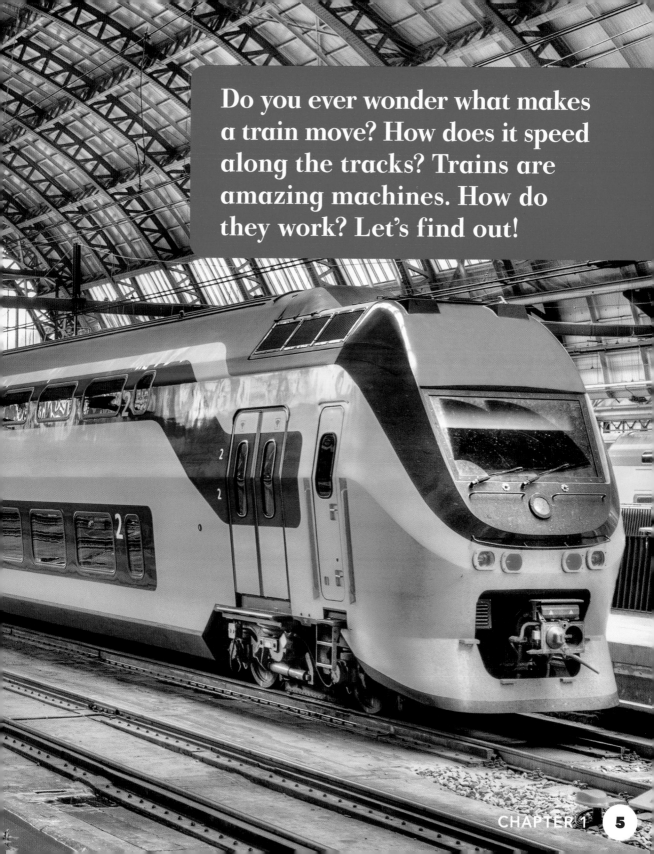

Do you ever wonder what makes a train move? How does it speed along the tracks? Trains are amazing machines. How do they work? Let's find out!

Steam **locomotives** pulled early trains. Water and steam powered them. How? Coal was burned in a firebox. This heated tubes in the boiler. Water around the tubes boiled. This created steam. The steam built up **pressure**.

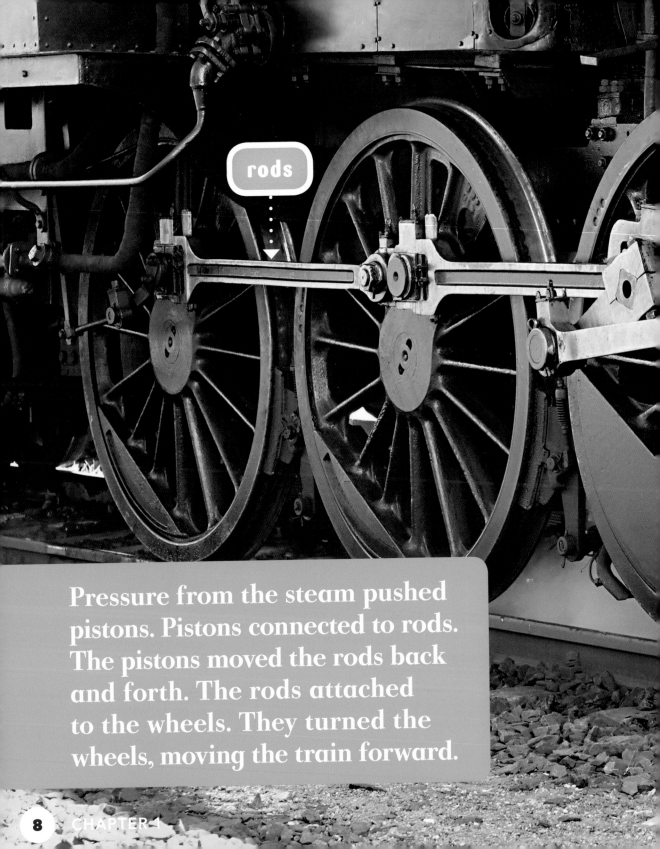

rods

Pressure from the steam pushed pistons. Pistons connected to rods. The pistons moved the rods back and forth. The rods attached to the wheels. They turned the wheels, moving the train forward.

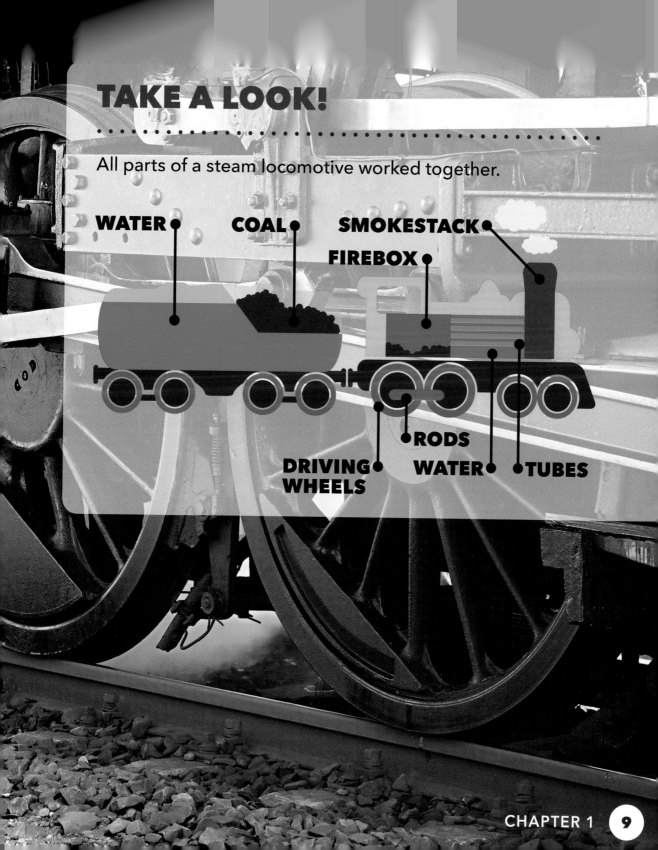

TAKE A LOOK!

All parts of a steam locomotive worked together.

WATER

COAL

SMOKESTACK

FIREBOX

DRIVING WHEELS

RODS

WATER

TUBES

CHAPTER 2

. . . .

DIESEL AND ELECTRIC TRAINS

In the 1940s, diesel locomotives became popular. They have **internal combustion engines**. This means **fuel** is burned inside these engines. This creates **energy**.

The engine spins an **alternator** to produce electricity. Electricity runs motors on the train's **axle**. This turns the wheels.

The largest kind of diesel locomotive was the Centennial. They were built between 1969 and 1971. Two diesel engines made them very powerful.

DID YOU KNOW?

Each Centennial was 98 feet (30 meters) long. They weighed 270 tons (245 tonnes)!

Not all trains have engines. Electric locomotives run on electricity. They get it from a third track. Or overhead wires power them.

How do trains stop? Air brakes. Each train car has an air tank. Pressurized air from the tanks pushes brake pads against the wheels. This **friction** stops the moving wheels.

DID YOU KNOW?

Trains also have manual hand brakes. They can be used if the air brakes lose pressure.

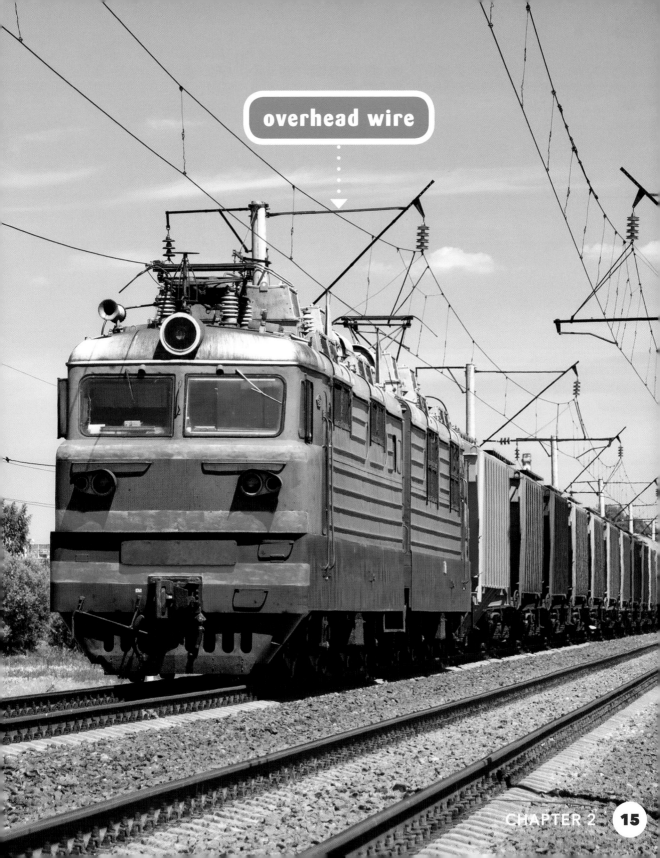

overhead wire

CHAPTER 3

MAGLEV AND HYDRAIL TRAINS

There are many kinds of trains. Maglevs are high-speed trains. Maglev is short for magnetic **levitation**. These trains do not have wheels.

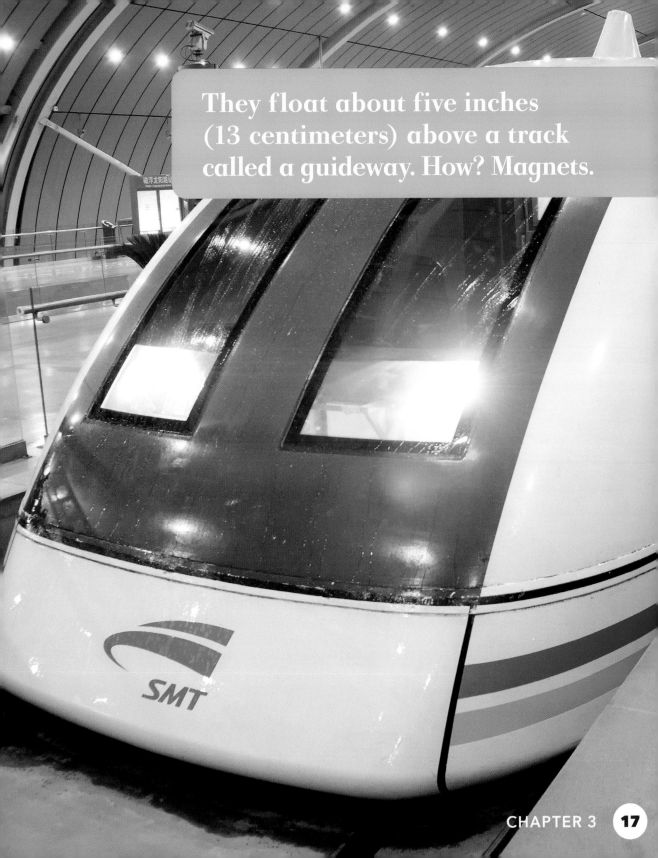

They float about five inches (13 centimeters) above a track called a guideway. How? Magnets.

There are magnets on the bottom of the train. They are also in the guideway. Magnets with like poles on the train and in the track **repel** each other. This keeps the train floating.

HOW DOES IT WORK?

Magnets also **propel** maglevs. Like poles are two north or two south poles. They repel and push against each other. Opposite poles attract. Both help move the train forward.

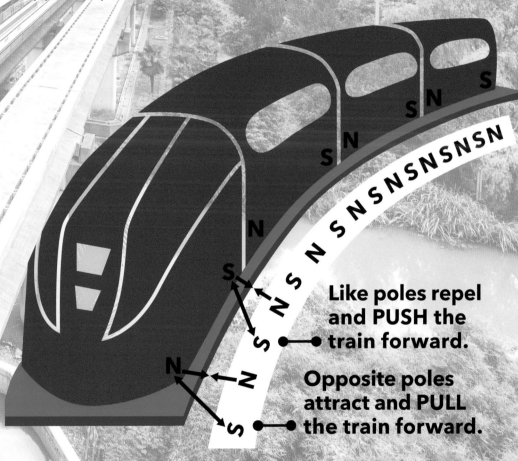

Like poles repel and PUSH the train forward.

Opposite poles attract and PULL the train forward.

The hydrail is the newest train technology. It is short for **hydrogen** rail. These trains combine hydrogen and oxygen to make electricity. Batteries store the electricity. The hydrail releases only water and steam. It does not cause air **pollution**. Maybe one day you will see one!

ACTIVITIES & TOOLS

TRY THIS!

FRICTION AT WORK

Find out how friction works with this activity.

What You Need:
- 3 or 4 small toy cars
- several thick books, enough to stack to about 1 foot (0.3 m) tall
- beach towel
- large piece of foam board
- masking tape
- yardstick

❶ Stack books under one end of the foam board to make a ramp.

❷ Line up all cars, side by side, at the top of the ramp. Hold them in place with the yardstick. Remove the yardstick quickly. Choose the two cars that raced down the ramp at the same speed.

❸ Place the beach towel smoothly over one half (left or right) of the foam board. Secure it in place with tape.

❹ Using the two cars you chose from the first race, place one on the rough, towel track. Place the other on the smooth track. Use the yardstick to hold them in place.

❺ Remove the yardstick so both cars start the race at the same time.

❻ Which car travels faster? Is it the one on the smooth track or rough track? Which track do you think has more friction?

GLOSSARY

alternator: A generator that turns mechanical energy into electrical energy.

axle: The rod or shaft on which a wheel or pair of wheels turns.

energy: Power that is used to operate a machine.

friction: The resistance when one surface rubs against another.

fuel: Something used as a source of energy.

hydrogen: A gas with no smell or color that is lighter than air.

internal combustion engines: Engines in which fuel is burned inside a combustion chamber.

levitation: The act of rising and floating in the air.

locomotives: Engines used to push or pull train cars.

pollution: Harmful materials that damage or contaminate.

pressure: The force produced by pressing on something.

propel: To push something forward.

repel: To drive back or push away against.

INDEX

TO LEARN MORE

Learning more is as easy as 1, 2, 3.

1) Go to www.factsurfer.com

2) Enter "trains" into the search box.

3) Click the "Surf" button to see a list of websites.

With factsurfer, finding more information is just a click away.